<u>Walking…Just Walking</u>

Walking ……Oh, the thrilling joy
of just slowly walking
Down the old dusty river road
along the snaking Rio Grande
My head held high enjoying
the cool morning freshness

Marveling at all natures wonderment
Watching the black vultures circling
in a powder blue clear sky

Graceful old muddy river winding through
all the majestic painted colored tall walls
of towering rocky mountain cliffs

Autumn rushes about this morning to leave
all of her subtle colors scarlet reds
different browns with splashes of yellows

Walking… Just walking

My stale night time lungs start to breath
in her coolness this refreshing morning

Its great to be alive to just breath
all of natures peaceful gifts

<u>Desert Blanket Peacefulness</u>

Thunder dark clouds billow
gathering in blues pastel lights
darks traces of gold outline
with sunset astounding
twilight reflection

Captive silent serenity for hours on display
hold back the dark gloved fingers of night
stretching touch of black velvet darkness

Scattering the Autumn twilight blanket
with amazing colored peacefulness

The Last Frontier

Always the refreshing desert wind
in my short Autumn hair

The soothing desert sunlight
on my now tan face and body

Blue fog draping it's long shadows
that are drifting high above the distant
Ghostly majestic Mountains

The Rio Grande morning muddy water
thunders down below me with speed
in the canyons below snaking
swiftly around rugged ridges
desert rocky earth browns
and coral rusty reds

I felt my mind for even more that day
with peaceful searching thoughts
as I slowly gaze across the always
endless desert vastness

Listening to the soothing songs
of desert birds and morning dove
gathering around for more
scattered wild bird seeds

High above me two red tail hawks fly
with grace in the refreshing cool
lifting morning breeze

Drinking my hot strong black coffee
finally I have now found peace
in my tattered ageing soul

I set outside watching dawning purple pinks
amazing stretching their golden fingers
with the breathless cool sunrise
with joyous happiness in my mortal heart

I smile and think to myself
how peaceful my heart has become
as I inhale the sweet desert scent now
starting a new glorious day

This place is called

The Last Frontier

The Big Bend Country

<u>Big Bend Country</u>

Unfurling dawn reaches out
with there essence scattering
its colorful inspiration miracle
palate of urging blissful
artist colors

Distant silence breaths coolness across
the desert vastness with peacefulness

Slight cool breeze playfully stirs
the desert green low bushes
the brilliant sun light captures
the lower canyons with different
dawning oils of colors

Spring floral bluebonnets of pastel blues
grace the winding roadways inside
the magnificent Big Bend Country

<u>Natural Sky Light Shadows</u>

My soul cries out for the night paper blue

natural wonder shadows of dawn face
My sable watching eyes skim slowly
across with the bright skyline

Yawning Morning how it entices the
insistence of another sunrise through
distant drifting painted clouds

It is urging with speed through the mystic
scarlet purple gold's rapture

Soothing wind with its healing eternity sky
and with all its glamour with temerities
Immemorial joys of pure radiance

My mortal heart leaps up with
a rainbow in the misty sky

Desert Vista

You will see in the pastel vast distance scrub
Creote with their green bushes
yellow native flowers that look
like vivid old Mexican blankets
on the majestic lower
sandy desert floor

Tasajilla cactus and leather stem bushes

every where with desert pink salt cedars
more snarled green mesquite trees
that reach out to embrace the day
with natures wonderment

Spanish Mexican daggers with
thick green blades and white blooms
very tall straight Sotol stalks
with cutting devil claws

Reach out from there rocky desert world
always peering out of the endless view

Scattered volcano mountains in the area
tiny chino summer grasses everywhere
spiny thorn yellowish Lechugilla
curved like a claw weapons

Desert Rain

What is that
Over in the distance shades of gray blues
With white puffs of other colors to blend

Gracefully the blue rain gathering shadows
were stretching over the desert butte
wetting its rocky pathway path

with raining gray fingers

On the wind-beaten desert rugged land
where once lived my Indian ancestors along
the snaking churning muddy endless river of
the muddy Rio Grande

Beneath the lazy hot after noon day sun
the hot spiraling dust rises into dirt devils
spiraling with the scorching heat
with the endless whispering wind

Dawning Moments

The dawning broke sultry and hot
after a massive sudden rain storm

Where the snarling desert cutting wind had
swept away loose soil leaving more stark
jagged rock formation with
its bare nakedness

Sunlight was striking the canyon rims
of lower canyons with light brilliance

Blue Mountains poked their wet heads
against the sweet painted vivid sky

Every thing seemed frozen for moments
to inhale slowly and enjoy the
wonders of this earth

<u>Mystical Twilight</u>

The waking sun looked out with
a distant lifting smile
behind the thick clouds
of colors display

The last brilliant sunset reaching rays
waved to me with her extending hands
of gracious sunset changing gold's

Twilight was with rapture silent
with her lady grace falling
clutching ebony night
fingers were stretching

The starry heaven stars
will become very close
darken with black velvet
above me

I must persuade myself to now listen
is it an echo of something
I must try to hear

This essence peculiar mystic spirit
with lingering final peace
I feel inside my soul

<u>Where Rainbows...Wait</u>

Tantalizing Comanche Autumn moon
with its endless embracing silent pleas

Will the pastel full moonlight shadows
browse along the canyon walls tonight
drenched in another mysterious glow

Let the frayed midnight silk of your mine
tear away in the whispering wind
one piece at a time and enjoy
this studded star silver

Let life's past stress blow away like dust
your unhappiness lay like old bones
to finally rest in peace
here arching pastel rainbows
wait for the stingy cool desert rain

<u>Desert Peacefulness</u>

Natures expressive sacred native face
strangely mingled with irrepressible
natural direction with it's
on conscious destiny

Over looking the desert rocky ledge
with so many thorny thickets
dusky red flowers bordered
a small running stream

Desert moss waving gently in the breeze
from their outstretched snarled limbs of
wild lavender orchard native trees

Wild pervading natures scent
on the whispering winds
skillful stole from the very breath
of stirring mesquite tiny leaves

Blue bonnets, Wild Sunflowers,
Indian paintbrush other blazing native
flowers patterned a very solitude
peaceful pathway through
stubby green sweet
summer grasses

Filling the evening afternoon atmosphere
with its wild desert stretching mysterious
amorous wild native perfume

She was breathing with her peaceful soul
her loyal sense of spiritual freedom
in the distance stood mountains
of shadows purple hues

Peaceful Land

The land here is so peaceful with
such amazing horizons ...

It is always changing in dawning lights
and with painted loyal sunset which
smooth out like scarlet red silk

All the rugged mountain edges harshness
so that everything flows
with faithful colors

My feet touch the earth wisdom knowing
it contains the birth of our spring life
and winters endless brutal death
I listen to the possession of itself
it is the season of my time to live

Desert Rainstorm

I listen to the talking sky with the vision
And chambers of my understanding ears

The ritual misty canyons
and distant mesa's welcome
the dawn with quite emptiness
with cold stingy rain incantation

More offerings against a gray blue
lightning sky my eyes see through
the endless dancing lightning
rain crashing with fury and clapping
Rolling vocal thunder that
echoes with his voice

I can feel the ritual rumble with strength
as it leaves my rainy world here
as plunges suddenly through
the endless space darkness

I can almost see the dawning light
starting my new life alone
but I am not afraid

The Desert Mysteries

Orange tangerine sun suddenly leaps
above the mountains heads freshening
another weaver spontaneous
ecstasy cheerfulness

Sweet is the desert dawning breeze
low fog lays low on the perfume floor

My heart is warm to the very core
with the morning pungent wind
in my ageing stale lungs

I feel the wet air on my cheeks
the desert silence is a courtesy
to my restless mind

Mysterious beyond the enshrined purple
The ghost mountains there is magic
in the sighing grateful murmurs

Dawn with its untarnished past ancestors
and how it lulls my mortal heart with
fragrant sudden spring flowers

<u>Dawning Freshness</u>

This tranquility scented living fragrance
the peacefulness reflected stillness

Dawning golden halo silence rising with
scent of sweet desert perfume wild blooms

Dawning spreading its silken pattern
With pastel colors like a straw mat
across the desert misty floor

The dancing sun plays hide and seek
On huge painted boulders and rocks

Billowing playful white clouds crowding
The sun torches as the cool breeze
flutters all around me as
I smiled to myself

I feel so loved and embraced
as life breathes happiness in
my stale night lungs

<u>Lavish Rainbows</u>

There is a pathway out of every
dark waiting shadow mist

Two rainbows arched and tucked
within the peaceful vastness

How it gives joy to our spirit

We must give our struggling heart wings
to fly chase our life dreams across
the endless happiness sky

Our love would have no rainbows
if our eyes had no crystal tears

<u>Saintly Peace</u>

The snarling systematic desert raging
wind was now violating
a white flag of truce
so merciless with clear native anger

Fate is flirtatious with hypnotic rage
if not to the natures brain there was
now the siege beyond

My Indian spirit instructed me

that I was never alone in the
unexpected waiting shadows

My mortal heart was suppose to be
a place of saintly freedom peace

Morning Rapture

Spring flowers rejoice when the long night
has left its nightly darkness pathway
they lift their sleeping heads
meeting the kisses of the
warm loyal sunlight

Hearing the soft cool hymn of the
whispering music in the drifting desert
Summer breeze as the birds flit
from branch to other high branches
with musical soothing notes

Light catching lingering shadows
on the canyons
below and across and dawning playful sky
with more swirling clouds of colors

Its freshness breathing cool desert air

into my very tired tattered soul
purity and peace taking away
the drab confusion in my life

Stingy Rain

The day swallowed the twilight shadows
the lightning branded the parched earth

Sudden wind stoke its crackling rusts
into multiply offering flames of pain

Blackest summer clouds with their
treacherous glare but the stingy
desert rain never came

Parched Thirst borders their domain

Desert Rubble

The fragile essence of my only heart
so divided with closer inspection

Disappointment crouching next
to forging thoughts as to why

Speaking out our world of now silence

the stretching fingers of night darkly
caress the ghostly distant mountains

Still I entrusted my heart in your hands
with only the March winds rattling
on the desert rubble you left

I sit outside patiently with the pastel fog
still with your silent grooming tongue
trying to hear what you don't say

Sunset light preens its shimmering
feathers tears trickle like crystals
in the shimmering reflection

Highest Mountain

Festival threading mounting dawning
colors taking ones heartaches
out of ones troubled misery
joy comes inside the
dormant soul

Golden sun and silver fragrant
rains standing on a very high
mountaintop watching the
silent mist unfold like
a velvet spring rose

Not even times loyalty can ever still
the cool lingering peaceful winds
that embrace my mortal thoughts

Stony Beds

To breath in and enjoy life every day
sudden nudge of the last intoxicating
gusting breath the traveling wind
on my mountain desert home

Red tail hawks sway with grace
with the uplifting warm drafts

The snaky river below my home
comes with rushing water
as fast as it leaves

Leaving her stone beds thirsty

Hiking Lower Canyons

Went hiking yesterday morning and ended
up walking down the old river bed
called, Terlingua Creek

Treasure of stones of every color
and every rock its own shape

I found myself making a pile of stones
to take back home and put in
my own cactus garden

Small rushing playful waterfalls cascading
over the shimmering countless polished
boulders with gurgling happiness

I looked up to just listen to the desert
with it fall colors of browns and yellow
still in the rustling cotton wood trees

Prickly pear cactus were every where

down low in the lower basin canyons
with the warm winter afternoon sun
still blooming it's pink wonder

Peacefulness in my body and soul
I walked slowly with the warm sun
on my tanned face and the
cool breeze playing with
my Autumn hair

<u>Desert Thunder Storms</u>

Echo voices of thunder faded
sometimes even becoming muffled
or lost in the cobalt evening summer blue
always changing turquoise sky

Purple undressed cotton candy feather
clouds spiraling with massive messenger
shades of pastel pink and soft grays

Distant boundaries a winter
thunderstorm bent close
to the blanket mountains

Anticipation rainbows whispering

among themselves gathering
moaning winds rushing
across the desert floor

<u>Panther Moonlight Canyons</u>

While I listened to the traveling wind
more silence came from nowhere

Stardust glass blue stars swarmed
black velvet the brighter large
ones dusty and hints of red
behind the small winking
against ebony curtains

For hours I drifted with my searching
night eyes where the old moonlight
canyons are worn into nothing but
evolution intricate endless shadows
standing with all eternity time
and crumbling boulder rocks

The massive sculpture hanging
its desert formation landscape
descended into abandoned silent
darkness gestured for me
to look more with extending
curiousness

A night panther screams came out
of the midnight darkness

<u>Whispering Desert Wind</u>

Shadows pretended to hide themselves
across the desert's interwoven landscape

Magic resides within the hidden canyons
and the night mesmerized me
With formation thoughts

Rugged spell binding stone monuments
sculptured with rain and raging wind
enclosed with natural grasses

Where no trees catch the passing sound
of the whispering desert wind

<u>Desert Life</u>

My hovering eyes now captive by the
surrendering land with transformation

Where poetic words are crouched down

to concentrate on the floral treasures
I had found through this maze

So easy I thought to be carried away

I was being taken by the land of colors
and irresistible songs of desert birds

My consumed native thoughts pausing
submerged and soaking into my
native skin with the passage
serenity desert wind

Lightning Storms

Twilight dusk brought beautiful heat
lightning thunders storms across the
majestic ghost distant mountains with
drifting black cascading
veil sheer rain curtains

The different lights hanging captive
in the clouds an immense kingdom
with its own natural peacefulness
above the landscape absorbing
the light of winking stars

It became so dark later and finally still
that the night shattered the moon

Waiting Desert Thrives

Desert sculptured mountains
as far as the eyes can see
Colors of natural paint a place
you can finally breathe

In the day time its very hot
where you dwell
Always twilight becomes
a wondrous spell

Desert mountains all artist vivid colors
the painted canvas sunset sets
in the loyal west

When it rains the earth leaves
its refreshing scented rest

The air is clean with a cooling
refreshing misty rain smell

So many people come here to live
to get out of the city hell

<u>Waiting for Rain</u>

Black velvet canopy of blue stars sparkle
above desert moonlight unique canyons
the sounds of several howling coyote's
in the distant desert wilderness

Slight murmuring refreshing cool breeze
distant thunder and zigzag lighting
dancing on the ebony horizon

Dawning will leave a path of wild flowers
and sprinkling raindrops fall
from the endless heavens
where rainbows arch
in the sky

A spiritual peaceful place where
Rainbows wait for precious rain

<u>Desert Puma</u>

She hunts in her own solitude under
cloak of twilight sparse darkness
well hidden in desert brush

Where she must exist amid the vast
with wind swept stark beauty
with her own surviving skill

And thorny cattails that reach out
through silent pathway canyons
and mesquite tangled thickets

Prickly pear cactus and lechuguilla
survive on dry canyon rims

<u>Moonlight ~*~ Canyons</u>

The exhausted night mistress laid herself
down beside the dawning loving horizon

Distant sighing mountains wrapped
himself all around her with love in his
embraced hands of golden clouds

The desert aching breeze hushed
suddenly its mourning as they lay
together in a snug lovers embrace

Interwoven together as one in the
enduring night web shadows

Native Desert Spirits

Walking through rocky boulders
strewn animals endless trails
desert cactus flowers in bloom
crack sandy rock in their defiant
to reach the sunlight

A place where the wind was torrent once
the endless years of stingy rain
Desert thunder echo's stampeding
down the limestone canyon walls
and agate cliffs of colors

Faithful are the native spirits that
remember after years of change
that sigh with peace and ease

Amidst the tall pastel mountains
through the shadiness clouds
severed by endless times
weaving colored hand

I feel the shuffle of the morning breath
that brief moment that just lingers

Sometimes wind touches my cheeks
like an understanding loving spirit
from so very far away

<u>Whispering Desert Rain</u>

Whispering desert rain repeats it's rumors
with cool wetness across hazy mountains
with trickling raindrop blue destiny

Copper sunset blazes through glistening
with Indian blanket colors that lay
with evening wondrous peace

Smoky purple wispy stretching clouds
clutching distant melting colors palate
on the glorious horizon oils canvas

Daylight weaves and unweaves heavenly
net and still it pursues its sacred patience
with the crimson radiant fate

Immortal existence trapped for lingering
moments the parched desert with sacrifice
willingness surrendered with
unimaginable glory

Bob Cat Canyons

Just below is the Comanche creek
their are several distant canyons where
small deep dark caves are homes
to the night hunters

There south west ridge of crumbling cliffs
with constant falling desert rocks
amazing earth tones of stubble browns
shades also of dark cobalt blues

Mexican Walnut trees among arroyos
where wild hogs red foxes and gray
squirrels always searching
out their native foods

Agava plants are very abundant along
the rocky jagged high ridges
and lower desert ranges

Time as its keeper the desert sculpture
has eroded away to leave only flat mesas
which are now just weathered
with hard rock lime stone

<u>Out Here</u>

Here you stop all ticking clocks
cut off all ringing telephones

Here no stop signs in your way
No red waiting lights to wait

Here no gridlock lock in traffic
no crazy people trying to
run over you

Here only vastness of rugged mountains
in rainbow pastel breathless hues
with curtain rain falling
in lower canyons

Here just watching the sunrise
in corals and golden pinks

Here our brilliant exploding sunsets
in blazing dusky orange reds
lavender purples that flirt
with wispy gray night
fingers embrace

Peaceful Desert

Shifting colors indelible fire- lighted
shadows has cloaked across
Autumn fringed with perfection
desert valley of blue mountains

Gathering up painted cool gusty clouds
the wind blows it's restless breath
changing shadows whisper
and then blow away

Mountain streams trickling babbling
echo's down through snaky sunlight
canyons colored with natural shades
of dusky red tans and brown creams

A slight mist lingers threading through
the majestic ghostly priestly distance
natures song bird melody
with soothing peace

Painted Wonderment

Crimson streaks across the colored
vastness of massive volcano rocks
and dusty dry sand

Cactus flowers and Spanish daggers
with flowering sweet yuccas
are all in Spring bloom
in this amazing peaceful
desert land

Rabbits sneak around the scrub bushes
and rocks in the late afternoon place

The coming of painted night can be seen
in the western night twilight space

The late sunset graces the last of colors
on the mountains of pinks and blues

The smell of sweet rain in the cool wind
of golden scarlet whispering hues

A wild native coyote can be heard in
the distant afternoon cool breeze

As the cool night sweeps down on
the hot desert with gentle ease

<u>Desert Walk</u>

Touching my face with painted sunshine
as it creeps up and over the range of
cobalt blue mountains

Spring morning desert breeze cools me
when I take long walks through tall
yuccas and perfume native cacti
summer sweet white blooms

I listen to the still peacefulness slowly
strolling through the colored volcano
scattered rocks watching out
for spiny low dog cacti

Jack rabbits running through
the low rattlesnake bushes
birds flit from Mexican swords
to near by old mesquite trees

Desert willows in the winding creek beds
wave in the scented sweet wind with grace
tiny purple perfumed wild orchards

I have finally come back home

Who...

Who thunders in the endless cathedral
mountains whispers with dancing rhythm
in the desert wet stubby grass
always running from the
stretching wind

Who flings rhapsody of sunset gold's and reds
across a soundless infinite twilight kingdom

Save the lonesome cry's of the evening doves
as desert dusk fell silently and still
with heaven peacefulness

I understand this rich redemption perfection
gathering the seamless golden threads
of dawns bronze hemline garments

Sculptured Mountains

Desert sculptured mountains
as far as you can see
Colors of natural paint
a place you can breathe

In the day time its hot where you dwell
Twilight becomes a wondrous spell

Desert mountains all the artist colors
the painted canvas sunset sets
in the loyal west

When it finally rains the wet earth
leaves it's refreshing scented rest

The air is so clean with such a cooling
refreshing misty rain smell

Out here in this desert they called us all
desert rats that thrive in this hot hell

<u>God Has Painting Fingers</u>

Tonight the seducing desert cool breeze is
breathing softly on my bare skin

Native birds happily singing
in the Spring yuccas

Spiny thorn cat claw bushes

that reach out with longing
snag anything that moves

The Majestic Ghost mountains with
twilight hues of whisper pinks
and stretching powder blues

Twilight colors paint the endless sky
with loyal colors of pale royal purples
and golden silken jagged lace edges
That outline the distant clouds hues

I sigh as Gods paints with his own artist
bold vivid painter fingers
Brilliant with every swirl of colors
and painted artist shape

<u>Dawn ~*~ Twilight</u>

The enchanting glory of another dawn
came with silent feet on shafts of golden-
guided light with its serenade
of singing native birds with
gathered happiness

Twilight's purpling smudging hue
enshrouds the distant vivid sunset

mountains with its cool shad
cloak of mysterious splendor

As shadows foretelling the peaceful
nightfall with subtle sweet
floral night fragrance

There in the loneliness of afternoon rain
faded into rainbow colors of evening
Earth unadulterated as graceful
as an eloquent nude

Desert Enchantment

There in the silent loneliness of another
sunset the rain -faded into mysterious
rainbow colors and Earth exposed
herself unadulterated
graceful as a eloquent
beautiful nude

The twilight's cool mist shrouded
the colorless sand as the soft spring
breeze sang symphonies of life

The silken evening was well dressed
in a veil commonplace with heavens
happiness tears as the silence bathed

in the sweet desert atmosphere
of twilight graceful shadows
mingling with colors
of approaching
night fingers

The desert vastness proclaimed its
essence with equal ecstasy
as my aching heart
quieted accepting
its royal beauty

The refreshing breath of a breeze
soothed my tired soul

<u>Outstretched Freedom</u>

Twilight sheds forth another evening
afterglow peacefulness pathway
to point the way to its
serenade beauty

This deliverance place heals my wound
with comfort and gladdens my
weary worn out heart

Many glorified embracing shadow
gather around me and capture it
majestic loveliness and grace

With its hint of subtle sweet fragrance
lingering near nothing as lovely a
Spring in the painted desert

<u>Peacefulness Weaves</u>

Royal purples and arousing playful pinks
its eloquence painted symphony
with her humble reverence
she nods her golden
dawning head

Ebony studded velvet curtains with her
endless persuasive silken spaciousness
stretching her sheer shadow gray's

The breathless sunset silence continues
neutral with the last amazing woven
refinements to amaze us all
with her loyal mystery

Translucence as a sheer veil with her
unforgettable fragrant sweet
freshness as the vapors
rises high in the endless
desert turquoise sky

Your Invisible cleansing night wind
I am so very enthralled by your
immersed warm embrace

Peacefulness weaves a silken garment
without evading coaxed love words

Glittering Tapestry

Old man winter will blow his frigid cold
north breath down through the Autumn
vastness as he lays glittering blanket
snow on the surrendering
desert mountains

His cold icy fingers were silently stealing
the colored brittle leaves from
the frozen branches

His cold breath roared out from blue lips
stopping all the running streams

And as he walked he froze all the grasses
into a diamonds of amazing tapestry

Then he lay down and curled up
and went sound to sleep

<u>Rainbow Mist</u>

Little drops of anguish all running
together like a cascading waterfall
over lifeless cliffs of high rocks
and mountain boulders

All water drops quench the endless thirst
of trailing graceful emerald vines
hanging and snarled heavy roots
clutching tightly to hold her

She was drenched with coldness
to the skin attacking water fury
didn't drowned her the graceful
rainbow mist admired
her fighting courage

<u>Desert Whispers</u>

My skilled artist hand now paints
landscapes of distant mountains and
desert rugged colored hills

My inspirations become the white
colored candy cotton clouds
floating stretching across
the towering vastness

My jeweled gold is the sunlight
that plays among the lower ridges
and latticed boulders of paints

Moonlight silver with its mystic sheen
spreading like sweet dressed
fragrant spring blossoms

Dawning brings me more added dewdrops
endless whispers of a free spirited breeze
with its captured peacefulness

Desert Blanket

Thunder clouds billow gathering
in pastel colored lights darks with
traces of gold outline the curved edges
with sunsets graceful loyal reflections

Scattering all the twilight autumn blanket
colors within the desert floor with its
amazing painted peacefulness
across the great vastness of

distant blue ghost distant mountains

Captive silent serenity on royal display
with its mysterious wonderment

Please hold back the very dark gloved
fingers of night with stretching
endless golden light

Twilight Dusted

Twilight distant massive mountains that
arched down below the Rio Grande river
that snake through the majestic
wall of towering canyons

The desert land with its essential silence
except for the cool wet wind dewdrops
that kissed the thirsty parched plants

Changing light collects tenaciously
in my eyes standing and admiring
the various sunset grasses
with shades of soft hues

Glistening with relentless sweet rain
leaving their comfort finger prints

Pastel Light and purple darkness
sliding through the emptiness

Poetic emotions plunging me
into peacefulness

<u>Whispering Desert Rain</u>

Whispering desert rain repeat
it's whispering rumors
with its cool wetness across
hazy blue mountains
with trickling raindrop
topaz destiny

Copper sunset blazes through glistening
with Indian blanket colors that lay
with evening wondrous peace

Smoky purple wispy stretching
clouds clutching melting palate colors
on the glorious oils and canvas

Daylight weaves and unweaves its
heavenly net and still it pursues
its sacred patience with the
crimson radiant fate

Immortal existence trapped for lingering
moments the parched desert with sacrifice
willingness surrendered with
unimaginable glory

Natures Breath

The parched earth thirsty for spring
soaking rains to wet her changing
mother land bosom with her
outstretched raining fingers
and cool refreshing hands

She will leave soon with warmer summers
days her radiance spring hair full
of yellow melting glow
sunlight evening leaves

Summer will serenade the teasing wind
with her emerald lively colors
across the land timeless nature
in her own flight

Upon the magnificent tallest mountains
and breathless waiting pathway
with sensual spirit breath

<u>Vivacious Wild Flowers</u>

Let the quite wind softly blow over me
watching the pastel shadows pass
under the blazing sunset

Swaths of many changing colors of gold
and corals waiting for the moments
as my mind responds
looking at this loveliness with sighs

Listening to the perusing soothing notes
of paused savoring musical conversation
under the artist light of desert twilight

Where soon the vivacious wild flowers will
drowse with warm night whisper
dreaming until the dawning birth of
another glorious day

Secret Canyons

Like lost cavern whispering winds that
echo through huge cliff walls it passes
through to the dreary waiting river
it's madness to proclaim

Willow trees hung as if deaf dead
skeletons to the clashing roar
of shield thunder lightning fingers
burns the land which now
remains dormant

Obedient through the lapse of remaining
time still its defiance pensive shades
appear with the noon-tide scorching sun

Deep inside the secret walls dwell the
answers then trembles in silence
as the day runs across the
endless vivid sky

Crying Desert

Rugged colossal distant cliffs were now
stretching into soft pastel graceful hues
with the evening native rapture paint
brush in artist colors

Sullen cries was testing the west torch
of heat it's blazing massive head wind
with burning breath rush

Silence reined this desert dry world
native plants who thrived with just
a few stingy drops
of saving rain

In shallow moist creek beds cotton woods
leaves rattled within dust devil breeze
with the lightning speed it had
suddenly gained freedom

Gathering huge white cathedral clouds
invade the sun's face performing clouded
shadows across vast desert painted floor

Evening promises cool taste of falling rain
to a crying desert always begging for
just a little bit more to drink

<u>Native Desert Wilderness</u>

Breathing desert floor now slowly
awakens displaying the wild stubby
grasses and sweet perfumed purple sage
dawning now with purple pinks rapture

Enclosed within her arms a circle of
colossal cliffs stretching with vivid
vermilion pastel hues of distant
baby blues and royal purples

A muddy river split's the dusty red walls
with breath taking rusty grandeur

When the shifting winds were from the
hot west a sullen roar it's somnolent song
murmured a restless whispering melody
through the rattling native
cotton wood tees

Little rain gathered with cathedral clouds
with a few stingy drops of cool rain
from time to time

<u>Twilight Dusted</u>

Twilight dusted the distant mountains
that arched down below to
the Rio Grande river

This desert land with its essential silence
except for the hot changing wind

Changing light collects tenaciously
in my eyes standing and admiring
the various sunset grasses

Glistening with relentless sweet rain
leaving their comfort finger prints

Pastel Light and purple darkness
sliding through the emptiness

Wild pervading scent on whispering winds
skillful stole the wild perfume of flowers

Blue bonnets all in Spring bloom
Indian paintbrush scattered
blazing wild flowers patterned
a solitude pathway through
the awakening summer
sweet short grasses

Filling the sultry evening atmosphere